London Transport Country Buses Part 1 - South

RT 3125 was photographed at Gadebrook Cross Roads on 9th August 1958 on its journey from Redhill to Dorking. This was the location where the routes 429 and 439 merged for the run to Dorking via Brockham. This bus survives in preservation.

Laurie Akehurst

Photographs from the Peter Mitchell collection

Published by Adam Gordon

Front Cover: A classic view of a Country Bus in the early 1960s. RT 3190 is seen on route 424 at Smallfield whilst running from running from East Grinstead to Reigate on 6th August 1961. The wooden bus shelter complete with an enamel iron bus stop sign which includes its location adds to this delightfully rural setting.

All rights reserved. No part of this publication may be reproduced, stored in a retrieval system or transmitted in any form or by any means, electronic, mechanical, photocopying, recording or otherwise without the prior permission in writing from the publishers.

ISBN 978-1-910654-28-6

Publication no.132

Published in 2020 by	Adam Gordon, Kintradwell Farmhouse, Brora, Sutherland, KW9 6LU
	Tel: 01408 622660 E-mail: adam@ahg-books.com
Designed and typeset by	Barnabas Gordon
	Tel: 07795 201 502 Email: Barney@ahgbooks.com
Printed by	4edge, 22 Eldon Way Industrial Estate, Hockley, Essex, SS5 4AD

RT 3397 en route from Tonbridge passes through Bessels Green on route 403 bound for Wallington on 30th September 1967. Long trunk routes such as this were a feature of the network and the passengers in the upper deck front seats are no doubt long riders, perhaps on Green Rovers, enjoying their trip.

AUTHOR'S NOTE

The photographs displayed in the book were all taken by Peter Mitchell and the vast majority have not been previously published. Peter Mitchell (1929 – 2011), a Rating Officer by profession, was an avid photographer of both road and railway transport and windmills. He started photographing seriously in 1949 and it is very fortunate that he recorded the date and location of all of his work. This information has been included in the captions except in a few instances of ambiguity. In certain cases the same bus may have been photographed on the same route on different days or at several different locations. With the aid of a car Peter was able to reach some of the more remote parts of the network and it is fortunate that he often made attempts to capture some of the more obscure workings.

This book covers the London Transport Country Area (South) starting in 1949 up until the cessation of London Transport's control of the system at the end of 1969. In addition, a few photos have been included from early London Country days before standards were allowed to drop and vehicles appeared in unsuitable liveries. Having rejected a geographical division between the south and north areas the former is defined as all routes numbered in the 400 and 850 series plus a few Green Line views. The photographs are presented in an approximate clockwise progression from Gravesend to High Wycombe. It has not proved possible to include a photograph of a bus on every route although a very good representation will be found. It is proposed to produce a comparable volume for the north area.

When Peter started photographing and recording in 1949, London Transport's Country Buses & Coaches required a maximum output of 1,176 vehicles. Peaking prior to the bus strike in 1958 at some 1,347 buses and coaches, a sad decline then set in and at the end of London Transport's control this figure had dropped to 1,115. In conclusion I would like to express my sincere thanks to Simon Butler, Barney Gordon and Hugh Taylor without whose valuable assistance the production of this book would not have been possible. Thanks must also go to Paul Ross who kindly read through the text.

Laurie Akehurst
Watford, October 2020.

Route 409 was another of the lengthy Country Area trunk routes in this case running from West Croydon to Forest Row. RT 4748 has the main road through Newchapel to itself on 2nd October 1965.

London Transport was impressed with the revolutionary Q type, the prototype of which had been delivered to the London General Omnibus Company in 1932. In 1935 an order for 100 buses, later increased by two, was placed for the 4Q4 version which was chosen to be the standard Country Area large saloon single-decker. Q 35 is seen in Gravesend town centre on the short local route 497 on 15th July 1951. Once a busy daily route with a 12 minute frequency, by the end of London Transport's tenure in 1969 just two Monday to Friday journeys were provided. The Co-Operative shops were once a familiar sight in high streets, offering cheaper produce than many other stores and also paying an annual dividend to members.

The LGOC and its associates had an agreement with Maidstone & District Motor Services fixing their boundary at Dartford and Farningham. Under the London Passenger Transport Act of 1933 the area of the new Board was extended eastwards to cover Gravesend and Wrotham. The trunk route over the Gravesend to Dartford section became numbered 480 on 20th November 1935 and gained an extension to Erith on 6th April 1938. The busiest Country Area route it was as frequent as every five minutes at certain times. Although officially converted to RT operation in October 1949 in this view taken on 1st August 1954 STL 1784 is seen in Gravesend town centre.

A number of rural routes ran to the south of Gravesend towards Longfield by various routeings, continuing to Ash, Hartley Court, Meopham and, at one time, to West Kingsdown. C 77 was one of a batch of 74 Leyland Cubs delivered in early 1935. The Cubs seated just 20 passengers which was the maximum number legally permitted for one-man operated buses at the time. The bus, nearing the end of its days, is seen on 1st August 1953 laying-over between trips on the Gravesend Clock Tower stand. Route 490 ran to Ash via New Barn.

Once London Transport had acquired various independent operators a major re-organisation of services took place in Gravesend on 16th May 1934. Other than odd extensions and enhancements for new housing over the years the route network was basically unchanged when the routes were handed over to London Country in 1970. This view was taken in Gravesend town centre on 15th July 1951 showing roof-box STL 1919 on route 495 running between Northfleet and Kings Farm Estate via Waterdales and Parrock Street. The bus, new in 1937, was painted green in March 1941 and taken out of stock in August 1953.

Companion route 496 also ran between **Northfleet** and **Kings Farm Estate** but via Vale Road and Windmill Street. STL 1648 went into service at Holloway Garage in November 1936 and received green livery in March 1944. Seen in **Gravesend** town centre on 15th July 1951 the bus is heading towards **Northfleet** showing the style of destination blind designed to show an indirect, in this case round the houses, type route. Having become a driver training bus STL 1648 was not taken out of stock until May 1955.

Gravesend was unique in the London Transport area in having at one time six special routes operating only at lunch times to allow workers at Rosherville to go home for lunch and return just within the hour. At shift start and finish times no such journeys were run and workers were obliged to walk to or from Overcliffe or Gravesend town centre. In this view taken on a very warm 7th August 1967 RT 3148 leads two other buses from Pier Road to Burch Road to pick up the hungry workers.

RT 2500, the last of the trio is seen in the same spot as RT 3148 working on the 487A to Alkerden Lane, Swanscombe, a run of 15 minutes. These special routes traversed certain roads not used by other routes and the buses waited approximately 25 minutes at each terminus before returning with the workers. In practice the routes were strictly for the workers and casual passengers were not conveyed. The Thames shipping in the background is seen in an era prior to the introduction of containerisation.

During 1965/6 the Country Area was allocated 100 RMLs to replace RTs on some of the busier routes. Northfleet Garage received a batch of 19 RMLs principally for route 480 from 21st November 1965. RML 2342 is working the 487A journey to Swanscombe on 1st August 1966 and is seen with few passengers in London Road, Northfleet. This bus spent its entire Country career at Northfleet until September 1979, eventually being sold back to London Transport before being finally withdrawn from Shepherd's Bush Garage in January 2004.

To the east of the town centre in Gravesend the Board's boundary was fixed at Denton which was served principally by routes 480 and 480A. The frequent service of Maidstone & District buses going further east were not allowed to convey passengers locally within the London Transport area. In this view a well-presented RT 3160 waits at the Milton Ale Shades terminus before returning to Rosherville on 7th August 1967. Some of the intermediate points blinds could show "Works Special" but evidence suggests that the conductors preferred to show the blank display.

A rare visitor to Northfleet Garage was RTL 852 which was temporarily drafted in on 24th July 1959 as part of a massive transfer of vehicles principally caused by stage three of the trolleybus replacement scheme. The transfer of some RTLs to Northfleet allowed 13 RTs to be released to Windsor to cover extra workings during August. The RTLs were restricted to the Gravesend local routes as they were not allowed to enter the Central Area on route 480. The bus is seen in Singlewell Road near Kings Road heading for Kings Farm Estate on route 488. Whether by accident or design Peter took this photograph on 4th August 1959.

The Leyland Cubs were replaced by the 26-seater GS class in late 1953 and early 1954. Route 451 linked Gravesend with Hartley Court via Betsham on which GS 48 is seen at Westwood, The Wheatsheaf while working a short journey between Gravesend and Fawkham Station on 4th August 1959. Fawkham for Hartley Station was on the former London, Chatham & Dover main line and during 1961 it was renamed Longfield for Fawkham and Hartley. The original Longfield Halt on the Gravesend West Street branch line had closed in August 1953.

The alternative route between Gravesend and Hartley Court was the 490 running via Southfleet and New Barn. GS 79 is seen in Earl Road, Gravesend heading for Hartley Court on 24th September 1960. This bus was allocated to Northfleet Garage from November 1954 until November 1962. Note the two request bus stop flags, one attached to a telegraph pole and one to a lamp standard.

Route 492 was introduced on 18th May 1949 consisting of just two or three journeys between Gravesend and West Kingsdown. A number of new rural routes were introduced across the system at this time but unlike the others the 492 did not cover any previously unserved roads. Never very busy the Wednesday service – early closing day in Gravesend - was withdrawn during September 1955 and complete withdrawal followed the six-week bus strike in 1958. GS 54 is seen on the stand at West Kingsdown prior to returning to Gravesend. The photograph was taken on 28th July 1958 exactly three months before withdrawal.

Route 489A linked Meopham (Hook Green) with Gravesend via Southfleet, a circuitous journey which could be made directly by Maidstone & District services. RF 658 is seen at Meopham (Hook Green) terminus on 30th April 1960. The 489A and companion route 489 to Ash were converted to one-man operation on 16th October 1957 and the bus carries the orange Perspex "Pay as you enter" sign that was introduced in 1960.

RF 580 is seen at Longfield Station on 25th July 1964 whilst working a journey to Gravesend on route 489A. This RF did not pass to London Country in 1970 but instead was one of thirteen Country Area RFs transferred to Muswell Hill Garage on 1st January 1969 for route 210. The buses initially ran in green livery but were eventually repainted red. An RT on route 423 stands behind.

RT 4191 stands in the pleasant surrounds of Singlewell terminus on route 487 before returning to Swanscombe on 30th April 1960. Certain journeys on the 487 had been extended from Gypsy Corner to Singlewell on 14th October 1959 in order to serve new housing at Hever Court Estate. Note the metal-framed bus stop flag on the LT-manufactured concrete post. At this time London Transport was fitting all buses with flashing trafficators – the bus has received the mountings but the trafficators themselves have not yet been fixed into position. This bus was exported to Iowa, USA in 1971.

Route 498 had been a special schools route in Gravesend in the mid-1930s and the number had been reused in 1952 when a route was introduced between the Clock Tower and Coldharbour Estate. On 13th May 1959 an additional leg of the route was provided between the Clock Tower and Painters Ash Estate. An immaculate RT 1105 is seen at Painters Ash terminus on 19th September 1964.

RT 4193 and RT 3424 make for an interesting comparison when seen on the stand at Northfleet, Plough on 30th April 1960. The former is fitted with the older style of via blind with five lines of intermediate points while RT 3424 has the newer four-line type progressively introduced from 1955. Unlike at some garages the engineers at Northfleet always looked after the blinds and many lasted longer than was normal for the fleet as a whole. RT 4193 has received trafficators unlike its companion.

RT 4170 is seen on route 495 in Perry Street heading for Northfleet via Waterdales on 24th September 1960. The uppercase intermediate points blind is both informative and pleasing in appearance. Few could have foretold by the end of the decade that this route would have been operated by high capacity single-deck standee vehicles. Following overhaul in 1969 this bus survived in red livery finally being withdrawn from Barking Garage in October 1978.

London Transport's Bus Reshaping Plan of 1966 was somewhat dismissive of the Country Area simply stating that one-man operation would be much extended. The negotiations to pave the way for high capacity driver-only vehicles were long and difficult and finally in the winter of 1968/9 Merlins using the Autofare system were introduced in various towns across the network. In Gravesend routes 495 and 496 were converted to MBS operation on 15th March 1969. A brand new MBS 425 was captured by the camera in Mitchell Avenue on 13th April.

RF 280 was a former Green Line coach which had been down-graded to bus status during 1965. The brackets for the side route boards have been removed and the seating capacity reduced by two to 37 due to the provision of luggage space. Route 450 linked Gravesend and Dartford by taking a rural run via Betsham and Bean before re-joining the main 480 route at Greenhithe. The bus is seen at Betsham, Colyers Arms where the route was joined by the 452 from West Kingsdown to Dartford. The London Transport fleet name is still carried although the photograph was taken on 31st January 1970.

The 452 was introduced in the May 1934 alterations linking Dartford to West Kingsdown running on Saturday and Sunday only. Other than the loss of the Sunday service during 1965 no change to the route had taken place when it passed to London Country – no doubt something of a record! RF 698 is seen at Fawkham Green on 31st January 1970. The bus started life as RF 647 and was fitted with a wider cab as one of the experimental RF one-man operated vehicles. In a complex renumbering exercise it became RF 698 on 26th January 1956.

The older order on the 452 is represented by T 447 which is seen in Priory Road, Dartford outside the garage on 15th July 1951. A former Green Line coach classified 9T9 and new to Dorking Garage in August 1936, with its ill-fitting window and damaged panel work the vehicle has clearly seen better days. It is in the war-time livery of white and green and was not withdrawn until August 1953.

Route 480 - the busy trunk route - was worked by Northfleet buses but from 2nd November 1955 odd supplementary journeys were provided by Dartford buses running to Stone, St. James Estate which was off the line of the main route. RT 2511 is seen at Horns Cross on 9th November 1970 with few passengers. The Dartford blinds were only equipped to show the route number, 480, and the destination with no appropriate intermediate points panel being provided.

RT 3426 is seen on 2nd December 1961 on diversion and has just turned off London Road, Dartford into Lingfield Avenue in order to reach Watling Street and Dartford town centre. This was possibly due to road works in connection with the construction of the approach road to the Dartford – Purfleet Tunnel.

The routes in Dartford were an interesting mix of long-distance trunk routes, local routes plus special services to various works and hospitals. There was a good deal of unscheduled duplication and unadvertised journeys at one time. In this view taken on 17th July 1954 STL 1784 is running between Dartford and Orchard Hospital on what should probably be a 423A journey. The bus is seen at the hospital gates. STL 1784 had been transferred to the Country Area during the Second World War and painted green in October 1944 and is seen here in its final all-over green livery.

A very well turned out RT 4195 heading for Joyce Green Hospital on route 423A is seen in Joyce Green Lane nearing the hospital on 30th September 1967. The bus is fitted with the less readable lower case via blinds which were progressively introduced across the fleet from late 1961. Although only a short run, unlike the 480 journeys to Stone, a proper via display has been provided.

Route 423B was provided primarily for the convenience of staff at the Thames-side Littlebrook Power Station. RT 599 stands in Langlands Drive at Watchgate, the Ladywood Road stand, on 19th September 1967. RT 599 was one of the first RTs to be allocated to the Country Area in 1948 when it would have had an earlier roof-box body. It lost the roof-box body at the end of 1959.

Route 423 was a busy route linking Longfield Station with Swanley Garage via Dartford. RT 4739 is seen here at Leyton Cross, Dartford Heath while running to Swanley on 23rd November 1963. The easily readable upper case via blinds were beginning to give way to the lower case style at this time.

Bow Arrow Lane was served from Dartford town centre by the short route 499 but when, in October 1954, the Sunday service was withdrawn, a Sunday pm service was provided as route 467A from Horton Kirby. RT 4515 was photographed on 17th August 1958 in St. Vincents Road, Dartford. The complex timetable was arranged so that the bus would return only to Wilmington where it would then work onto route 491. Route 467A was a casualty of the bus-strike, being withdrawn in October 1958.

RT 4525 stands at Horton Kirby terminus on 9th July 1966. Having arrived as a 467 the bus will return as a 491 and the conductor has set the side blind for the next journey. The London Transport concrete stop post and older-style flag complete the delightful rural scene. RT 4525 has only four months life ahead of it as a Country bus as it became a red bus upon overhaul in November 1966.

In stark contrast this view of RT 3212 was taken at Lower Belvedere on 30th April 1960 on the start of the route to Horton Kirby. Thames-side industrial buildings may be seen in the background together with some surviving trolleybus traction standards, some of which now function as street lighting poles. The trolleybus route serving Belvedere was the 698 which was withdrawn after 3rd March 1959 in phase one of the trolleybus conversion scheme.

Dartford Garage was something of a stronghold for STLs which latterly were employed on works services, finally being displaced on 11th August 1954. Shortly before this date STL 2071 is seen standing at the garage in Priory Road. The bus was new to Athol Street Garage in April 1937 and was fitted with a STL16 green-liveried body in March 1949.

Route 486 had been introduced on 26th March 1947 running from Dartford, Fleet Estate to Belvedere through some previously unserved roads between Dartford and Bexleyheath. RT 4531 is standing at the Fleet Estate terminus in Hesketh Avenue on 23rd October 1965 before departing for Upper Belvedere. The painted garage code and lower case intermediate points blind are typical of Country Area RTs in the latter half of the 1960s.

RT 4113 is seen at the same location on Sunday 25th August 1963 heading for Joyce Green, Orchard Hospital. The route number 475 is spurious as it should be 486A which made just one return trip on Sunday afternoons. Possibly the correct number cannot be shown so the conductor has displayed 475 (Crayford Ness works journeys) in order to distinguish the journey from the normal 486. RT 4113 passed to London Country but was sold back to London Transport in 1972 finally being withdrawn from Bromley Garage in August 1975.

Dartford Garage had its first RFs allocated on 28th April 1954 when cross-country Green Line coach route 725 Gravesend – Windsor, was strengthened over the Dartford – Windsor section. Dartford's RF 286 is seen passing road works at Worcester Park Station while heading for home.

Further RFs came to Dartford Garage when route 486 was converted to one-man operation on 15th February 1969. RF 560 is seen heading for Dartford in Burnham Road near Crayford Marshes on 9th August 1969. By this time transfers had replaced the "Pay as you enter" slip boards. Having subsequently spent some time at other garages RF 560 was withdrawn from Dartford Garage in June 1975.

From 15th May 1966 existing route 499 between Dartford town centre and Bow Arrow Lane was absorbed by a rerouted 486. A completely new version of the 499 commenced running between Downs Estate, the town centre and Temple Hill Estate where a vast loop was worked in both directions. RT 3185 is seen standing at the Downs Estate terminus in Teesdale Road on 9th July 1966. The crew have correctly set the blinds which could have been designed with a little more forethought to denote the circuitous nature of the route.

On the same day RT 3115 is seen in Henderson Drive, Temple Hill Estate while performing a clock-wise loop short working back to the town centre. No provision for stand time was made at Temple Hill Estate which accounts for the somewhat confusing blinds.

Red RT 2039 has been drafted into Dartford to work a railway replacement service on 30th May 1959. A specially prepared slip board displaying Farningham Road has been fitted. The bus is on loan from Plumstead and is seen outside Dartford Garage.

The lengthy route 401 linked Belvedere with Sevenoaks with a running time of 90 minutes. RT 4110 is seen at the Eardley Arms, Upper Belvedere stand in Heron Hill on a cold 20th February 1965. Swanley worked the largest share of the route and Dartford and Dunton Green buses could also be seen.

In order to serve new housing development in the Bexley area route 401A was introduced on 9th October 1963 shuttling between Bexleyheath and Joydens Wood Estate. An immaculately turned out RT 1728 approaches the original terminus in Woodlands Park on 29th August 1964. The front route number displays the number 401.

The same bus is seen waiting at the departure point. It should be noted that the front adverts were always a matching pair but this practice was not extended to cover the rear upper panels. Later in 1964 the route was further extended within the estate to Fernheath Way.

Routes 477 and 477A provided a service from Temple Hill Estate in Dartford to Orpington with projections on to Chelsfield. RT 3734 is in Littlebrook Manor Way, with Littlebrook Power Station in the background, on 16th March 1963 while working a short journey to Crockenhill on route 477A. The number 477A fell out of use in May 1966 when the section to Temple Hill Estate was taken over by the 499.

Swanley's RT 1728 is again seen this time in rural surroundings at Chelsfield Five Bells terminus on 18th June 1967 before returning to Dartford on route 477 after the route was curtailed at Dartford Garage.

Route 479 was one of the rural routes introduced in the post-war period serving roads which had previously never been provided with a bus service. It ran from Dartford to Farningham via Darenth, a route rendered impossible to follow today due to motorway construction. C 7 was new in 1935 and is seen still in the wartime green and white livery in Priory Road Dartford on 18th November 1950 between trips. Replaced by the GS, class C 7 finally went out of stock in September 1954.

The **GS** (Guy Special) class was ordered to replace the C class on one-man operated services. They were basically a standard model but with some London Transport adaptations. In this view Swanley's GS 13 is seen heading for Farningham near Horton Kirby. Dwindling numbers of passengers meant that the route was withdrawn in October 1958 in the massive cuts which followed the six-week bus strike.

Route 478 linked Swanley with Wrotham but other than on Brands Hatch event days passenger numbers were small. Local fares had been introduced on the parallel Green Line route 703 in 1956 and the number of journeys run on the 478 had fallen over the years. RT 1065 is seen at West Kingsdown on 23rd November 1963 returning to its home garage. The 478 was withdrawn in May 1964 with the 423 providing odd journeys south of Swanley.

The reinstatement of Green Line services in 1946 saw route 703 linking Amersham with Wrotham but the severe cuts of 4th November 1964 saw the 703 withdrawn and the southern section covered by an extension of route 717 which was converted to RMC operation at the same time. Just days after the change on 7th November, RMC 1492 is seen at County Gate, Foots Cray Road en route from Welwyn Garden City to Wrotham. By this time the front air intake grille had been modified and the off-side route number blind box painted over.

With expansion of services in the mid-1950s the Country Area became close to running out of available route numbers in the 300 and 400 series so the decision was made to introduce an overspill series in the 800s for northern routes and 850s for southern routes. Route 854 was introduced on 16th October 1957 forming a circular service in both directions linking Orpington and Chelsfield. Dunton Green's RT 3149 is seen at Chelsfield Station on 23rd April 1958.

The 854 was subsequently extended to serve Ramsden Estate and upon conversion to one-man operation on 31st December 1966 the opportunity was taken to renumber the route 493. RF 661 is seen in Tintagel Road, Ramsden Estate whilst proceeding to Chelsfield Station on 4th February 1967.

The 431 group of routes linked Orpington with Sevenoaks and also provided works journeys to and from Fort Halstead. Former Green Line coach RF 243 is seen at Orpington Station on 19th September 1967. The bus still carries the orange Perspex "Pay as you enter" slip board.

Fort Halstead was a top-secret government establishment situated north of Dunton Green and for many years was not even shown on maps. A series of local routes served the establishment at shift start and finish times. RT 3433 is seen near the exit at Polhill Arms taking home-going workers to Sevenoaks on 7th August 1967. These journeys were originally numbered 402 but from 31st December 1966 ran as 431D.

RT 3423 stands at Knockholt Pound terminus after performing the short run from Fort Halstead via Otford Lane as route 431B on 30th September 1967. At certain times prior to this the buses had run without route numbers simply displaying "Fort Halstead Works Special" but the route numbers were reinstated.

Route 471 was a rural circular linking Orpington with the villages of Cudham, Knockholt and Pratts Bottom running in both directions. GS 27 is seen near Cudham on an unrecorded date some time in the 1950s. The destination blind is designed to show the circuitous nature of the route.

The 471 retained its GS allocation until the end of 1966 but due to a partial conversion of the 431 group to RF one-man operation on 31st December 1966 it also received RFs at this time. RF 239 is seen at Green Street Green just after the conversion on 4th February 1967.

Following pressure from the Orpington Rural Transport Association, London Transport introduced route 479 running from Biggin Hill to Oprington on 16th February 1963. Running for just 18 Saturdays the route was withdrawn after 15th June and one week later the Orpington Rural Transport Association started their own operation. GS 19 is seen at Holwood Farm in Shire Lane near the junction with Downe Road on 30th March 1963.

Dunton Green Garage retained STLs for the supplementary schedule, which consisted mostly of Fort Halstead works journeys, until 31st August 1954. In this view taken on 7th August of that year green STL 1788 stands next to red STL 2049 in the garage yard. Both buses were delivered in 1937. Certain garages fitted STLs with full blinds towards the end of their lives and STL 1788 has been so treated.

STL 578 was new to Hackney Garage in October 1934 and despite being transferred to the Country area has retained its red livery. It is seen outside Dunton Green Garage on 4th November 1951. The bus was withdrawn in October 1953.

Route 454A was a variant of route 454 from Chipstead to Tonbridge running via Sevenoaks Station instead of Bat & Ball. Smartly turned out RT 3530 is seen on the Sevenoaks Station stand in Hitchen Hatch Lane on 7th August 1967. The bus displays the via blind for the parent route 454. These routes were destined to be amongst the last RT-worked at Dunton Green succumbing to one-man operation on 25th March 1972. This bus survived well into London Country days being withdrawn from Garston Garage in January 1977.

Somewhat surprisingly the rural route 421 from Sevenoaks to Kemsing and Heverham retained RTs until 1972. The route had been acquired from West Kent Motor Services in October 1939 originally being worked by 20-seaters. RT 3723 is seen at the remote Heverham terminus on 13th December 1964.

One of the last new Country Area routes to be introduced by London Transport was the 421A linking Sevenoaks and Otford via Sevenoaks Station which commenced on 29th September 1969. The peak hour route was provided primarily for employees of Mobil Data Services Ltd. working on Vestry Estate. RT 3160 is seen laying over at Otford Pond on 30th October 1969.

Routes 413 and 413A also came about because of the take-over of West Kent Motor Services. Route 413A ran from Four Elms to Chipstead through some lovely Kentish countryside. Crew operated RF 651 is seen at Toys Hill heading for Chipstead on 19th April 1958. The bus is off the normal line of route, possibly due to road repairs taking place between Four Elms and Ide Hill. The days of conductors enjoying undemanding duties such as this were numbered as the routes were converted to one-man operation on 23rd July 1958

The West Kent Motor Services' route had run through to the obvious traffic objective of Edenbridge but the Board's boundary prevented such operation. The 413A originally terminated at Scollops Road, south of Ide Hill, but on 6th July 1949 the route was extended to Four Elms Cross Roads where connections could be made with Maidstone & District. In September 1967 the terminal working in Four Elms was performed in service which meant that passengers could be carried to and from Chartwell Lane. Former Green Line RF 251 is seen at Chartwell Lane terminus on 7th June 1969, six days before the complete withdrawal of the route.

One of the most curious operations in the Country Area was the extension of two journeys on Sunday mornings beyond the normal terminus at Chipstead along otherwise unserved roads to Chevening Church. This was to allow local people to attend the church service. RFs on routes 413 and 413A had worked the journeys for many years but with the gradual curtailment of Dunton Green's one-man services on a Sunday it eventually became necessary to work these journeys with an RT. RT 4744 is seen at Chevening Cross Roads running to the church to pick up the home-going worshippers on 18th June 1967. Upon arrival at Chevening the driver has set the destination blind for the return journey and the conductor assists with the reversing movement. The Chevening journeys were withdrawn after 29th September 1968. The bus survived with London Country being withdrawn from service at Chelsham Garage in March 1975.

40

Route 413 linked Brasted with Chipstead somewhat circuitously via Ide Hill, Sevenoaks and Bat & Ball. From 9th October 1963, however, certain Sunday and evening journeys were rerouted at Bat & Ball to run to Shoreham Village to cover reductions on route 404. A very smart RF 686 stands at Shoreham Village terminus on 9th July 1966. The layout of the lower case style destination blind is quite pleasing. In the second view RF 686 is seen at Twitton railway bridge earlier on the same day working on the 404 from Sevenoaks to Shoreham Village.

In this extremely rare view of a **GS** working on route 404 **GS 21** is seen at Shoreham Village terminus on 28th July 1958. Dunton Green had a **GS** allocation for route 471 at the time and there was no cross-working between the two routes. The most likely explanation is that the **GS** is substituting for an **RF**. Routes 404 and 413/A had been converted to one-man operation just five days before so there could have been a temporary shortage of one-man equipped **RFs**.

42

The 402 provided a main trunk route from Bromley to Sevenoaks and Tonbridge but suffered a sad decline in passengers over the years with the service south of Sevenoaks eventually running only during Monday to Friday peak hours. RT 1616 is seen in Farnborough on 1st August 1966 performing a short journey to Sevenoaks. The decline in passengers was such that one-man RFs took over the route on 15th February 1969.

London Transport's operation extended outside the special area where Green Line coaches were granted restricted running rights to Tunbridge Wells - a very popular destination with day-trippers. In this view taken on Good Friday, 11th April 1952, Q 49 still in the war-time green and white livery stands at Tunbridge Wells Coach Station having performed a relief working from Victoria.

The other Country Area route from Bromley was the 410 to Reigate which required the use of low-height buses due to a low bridge at Oxted Station. From 1934 until replaced by the RLH class the route was worked by the famous, so-called, 'Godstone' STLs. Officially coded 11STL7 these buses were a batch of 12 which were the first new buses to be delivered to the Country Area. STL 1044 stands at Bromley North Station on a short working to Biggin Hill on 19th November 1949.

London Transport urgently needed more low-bridge buses during the Second World War and a batch of 20 bodies was built in 1941. Coded STL19 they were all fitted to earlier chassis replacing bodies lost through bombing. Initially all were painted red but STL 2250 was repainted green and white in June 1946 and is seen at Bromley North Station on route 410 on 16th September 1950.

STL 2311 is another STL19 type which gained Country Area livery in November 1944. This bus has subsequently been repainted in the green all-over livery apart from the between decks band. It is seen at Oxted Station east side on 28th July 1951 heading for Reigate and was taken out of stock in April 1953.

The route 410 was the first to be worked by the RLH class from Autumn 1950 until a diversion in Oxted in November 1964 allowed full height buses to be used. RLH 45 is seen passing Limpsfield Common bound for Reigate on 22nd September 1962. This particular bus was one of the lucky ones to survive long enough to pass to London Country Bus Services and was sold to City Coach Lines of Upminster in January 1971.

RTs took over on the 410 from 4th November 1964 but their reign was destined to be short as they were replaced by RMLs from 3rd October 1965. In this view RT 3147 is seen approaching Biggin Hill on 2nd October, the last day of official RT operation on the route.

From 10th July 1966 certain summer journeys on route 706 were extended beyond Westerham to Chartwell, the recently-opened home of the late Sir Winston Churchill. RF 57 was one of 175 RF coaches refurbished during 1966/7 and is seen in the pleasant surroundings of Chartwell on 30th September 1967. The journey to Aylesbury will take three hours and 31 minutes.

RF 243 stands at the Gresham Road terminus near Oxted Station east side on an inclement 8th December 1962. The coach is allocated to Tring but the length of route 707 was such that duty schedule constraints did not permit the Tring crews to work south of Chelsham. Certain coach duties at Chelsham were designated 'Tango' and just involved crews working a number of journeys either to Oxted or Westerham and back. Note the splendid coach compulsory stop flag.

The Westerham, Oxted and Edenbridge area was famous for three Cub-operated routes 464, 465 and 485 with at the time of this photograph Chelsham Garage supplying eight buses. C 82 is seen in Old Oxted on 24th May 1953 where the street has been suitably decorated for the forthcoming Coronation. This bus was one of a batch of 22 vehicles built for the Central Area in 1936 and was not released from stock until September 1955.

C 19 was one of the earlier Leyland Cubs, a batch of 74 being built for the Country Area in 1935, and is seen in Edenbridge on 28th July 1951. The bus is in the war-time green and white livery and unlike some members of the class has retained its front bumper. The 465 linked Edenbridge with Oxted a section of route covered by Green Line coaches until the outbreak of the Second World War.

The GS type took over from the Cubs in late 1953 and served the area well for another nine years. GS 81 is seen at Marlpit Hill at the north end of Edenbridge on 18th April 1960 while nearing the end of its journey on the 465. The timetable was arranged that upon arrival at Edenbridge the bus would depart as a 485 to Westerham.

The introduction of Routemaster coaches in 1962 allowed the displaced RF coaches to be cascaded to bus duties. Rather than convert more routes to one-man operation there was a move to use them to displace the GS class. Accordingly Chelsham lost its GS allocation from 24th October 1962 when RFs took over. RF 311 is seen on the 464 in Tanhouse Road between Oxted and Holland on 10th August 1963. This bus started life as Country bus RF 530 but was renumbered in 1956 when it was upgraded to Green Line status.

On Spring Bank Holiday Monday 3rd June 1968 a supplementary crew-operated RF service started on route 403 running between West Croydon and Chartwell. Running Sundays and Bank Holiday Mondays only it was withdrawn, never to reappear, at the end of the 1968 summer season. RF 684 is seen heading for Chartwell at Beech Farm, just south of Worms Heath, on 1st September 1968.

The long-established trunk route 403 linked Wallington and Croydon with Chelsham and an hourly projection continued through to Tonbridge. Due to curtailments on the Green Line south of Chelsham from 15th February 1969 the Tonbridge service was rerouted to double run via Tatsfield. RT 4508 is seen at Tatsfield, heading for Wallington, on 17th April 1970 in early London Country days.

In addition to the main route 403 the 403A ran from Wallington to Warlingham Park Hospital and the 403B to Farleigh. In this view taken on 6th September 1958 RT 2257 stands at The Harrow terminus in Farleigh prior to departing for Wallington. The bus retains an older via blind which shows five lines of intermediate points.

In this view of RT 1074 taken at West Croydon on 27th April 1963 the bus shows the corresponding four-line blind display on which South Croydon has been omitted. The stopping arrangements at this location would shortly be revised with the opening of West Croydon Bus Station later in the year. RT 1074 became a red bus in December 1965 and following withdrawal in August 1976 saw further service with Blue Diamond Coaches of Harlow.

Linking Chelsham and Warlingham with Caterham on the Hill the 453 was essentially a suburban route. RT 2259 is seen passing a small Austin van in Hillbury Road near Upper Warlingham Station on 13th March 1965. The route had been introduced in 1934 to serve new housing development in the area.

The service into Croydon was so busy that express journeys, which served only a limited number of stops, were run on the 403 between West Croydon Bus Station and Warlingham or Chelsham. The service was unusual in that the journeys were run dead against the peak flow. RT 4763 complete with white on blue blinds is seen outside Chelsham Garage on 7th August 1967.

With the withdrawal of Sunday services on some of the more rural routes the opportunity was taken to convert certain RT-worked routes to one-man operation on Sunday. Route 453 was so treated from 7th October 1965. In this view RF 547 is seen at a somewhat deserted Warlingham Green on 1st September 1968. This was somewhat typical of Sundays in a period when the shops were closed on that day. The stops here have been split with the Croydon-bound routes stopping at the far one and the 453 and Green Line coaches stopping at the near one.

In addition to the 403 group of routes from Chelsham into Croydon route 408 ran to Guildford and route 470 to Dorking. Chelsham's RT 4330 has just passed Trinity Church in Cheam Road, Sutton on its way to Dorking on 26th October 1967. This once-pleasant suburban scene is now part of the Sutton town centre one-way system.

RT 3154 is seen on companion route 408 further to the west in Cheam Road near the junction with Landseer Road on 8th March 1964. The running time from Chelsham to Guildford was two hours and 16 minutes which was an ideal journey for a trip out on a Green Rover.

Route 411 linked West Croydon and Reigate via Godstone and had been introduced in 1935 when short journeys on routes 409 and 410 had been linked up across Godstone. The older order is represented here by a splendidly turned out RT 3162 seen at Old Coulsdon on 6th August 1960. The bus was allocated to East Grinstead and cross-working from route 409 results in it appearing on route 411.

The new bus station at West Croydon opened on 31st July 1963 and was a considerable improvement over the previous arrangements. There was little activity at the bus station on 10th August 1966, a Sunday, when RML 2308 was about to depart for Godstone on route 411. The Godstone routes 409, 410 and 411 were the first in the Country Area to be converted to RML operation on 3rd October 1965. The use of the larger capacity, 72-seater buses enabled five buses to be saved due to the conversion. In some cases known inadequacies in the service were factored in to such conversions.

Godstone's lesser-known route was the 482, a special service for hospital visitors, which ran from Caterham Station to Smallfield Hospital on Thursday and Sunday afternoons. RT 995 is seen on the return journey in Smallfield Road, Horley approaching the junction with Balcombe Road on 26th September 1965, the last Sunday prior to the conversion to RML operation. The bus was transferred to High Wycombe once the RMLs took over.

Godstone Garage was the terminus for part of the service on Green Line route 709 to Chesham. The Amersham crews took their meal relief at Caterham and were only known to have worked right through to Godstone on Christmas Day! T 533 stands on the forecourt of Godstone Garage before departing for Chesham on 28th July 1951. New to Swanley in May 1938 the 10T10-classified coach was withdrawn in August 1953. Note the double bus and coach stop flag in the background.

RF 81 stands in the same location as T533 on 13th March 1965. In an unsuccessful attempt to make Green Line more attractive, route 709 was revised on 4th November 1964 to run express between London and Amersham using Western Avenue instead of the Uxbridge Road. From 31st October 1965 the route was withdrawn north of London just running from Godstone to Baker Street. Note the white on blue limited-stop slip board.

Route 708 from Hemel Hempstead to East Grinstead offered an alternative facility to the 709. RF 146 is seen on 7th October 1962 approaching South Godstone near the entrance to Posterngate Farm. This coach was one destined to be refurbished and was not withdrawn from service until March 1977.

East Grinstead has been linked to Oxted by route 494 which was introduced on 7th January 1948, one of a number of rural services provided at the time. Down-graded Green Line RF 59 is seen headed for Oxted on 29th January 1966 in Tandridge Lane at Chathill. The bus stop and finger-board sign posts are typical of a period remembered with affection by many.

The long-established cross-country route 434 linked Edenbridge with Horsham via East Grinstead and Crawley. In this view Q 70 is seen at Dormansland, The Plough, while working from Edenbridge to Crawley on 28th July 1951. The 4Q4 was new in October 1935 and lasted until July 1953 when it was displaced by a new RF.

From 19th May 1948 certain journeys on route 434 were rerouted away from the main road through Edenbridge to serve the remote community of Troy Town. RF 626 was photographed at Troy Town on the long run to Crawley on 21st October 1961.

Also seen at Dormansland, The Plough, but this time on 7th September 1969 are RF 254 on route 428 and RF 672 on route 473 which was a variant of the 434 running via Rowfant instead of Crawley Down. Route 428 ran from here to East Grinstead via Lingfield and Baldwins Hill.

The older order on route 428 is represented by STL 1739 seen at East Grinstead, The Crown, on 4th August 1952. The route was soon to receive surplus RLHs in October 1952 although no low bridges were involved. RTs took over from the RLHs in May 1955 but declining numbers of passengers meant conversion to RF(OMO) in October 1958.

An hourly projection south of Godstone saw the 409 running via East Grinstead to Forest Row in East Sussex. The buses set down passengers at the Swan in Forest Row and then continued dead to stand at the station which was on the line from Three Bridges to Tunbridge Wells West. RT 4748 is seen at Forest Row Station on 2nd October 1965, the last day of scheduled RT operation on route 409. The front destination box has been fitted with a narrower rear box blind and part of the glass has been obscured.

East Grinstead local route 435 to Imberhorne Estate was introduced on 9th December 1964 having been deferred from 4th November due to objections from estate residents who did not want a bus service. RF 551 stands at King Street Bus Station between trips on 13th March 1965. This photograph shows a Country bus RF at its best with the orange "Pay as you enter" slip board on the front and the double depth board on the side.

Route 435 also saw RT operation which was probably to provide work for the crews between other trips rather than for any significant passenger demand. Still smartly turned out RT 3211 was captured in Garden Wood Road under London Country auspices on 13th July 1972.

Route 424 linked Reigate to East Grinstead with variations in routeing either side of Horley. The route was scheduled to be worked by 4Q4s until June 1952. Q 55 is standing in Birkheads Road at Reigate Station before departure to East Grinstead on 23rd March 1952. The bus was new in September 1935 and withdrawn in June 1953.

10T10s were drafted on to route 424 in June 1952 as they in turn had been displaced from Green Line duties by RFs. T 607, one of the 34-seaters, is seen in Cockshot Hill Reigate heading for East Grinstead on 25th May 1953. New in July 1938 T 607 went to Northfleet garage and was withdrawn in September 1954.

As part of London Transport's initiative of running to previously unserved locations a supplementary service had been introduced on 11th August 1948 from Horley to Outwood. In other parts of the network even a minor deviation from the normal route was allocated a suffix letter but this was not the case with route 424. T 787 is seen this time at the Outwood Common terminus with the windmills in the background on 28th July 1958.

The main 424 route was converted to RT operation in May 1955. In this view RT 3216 has just left the Stone Quarry Estate terminus in East Grinstead and is seen in Holtye Road on 4th August 1959. In addition to the main route and the shuttle services there were also special journeys between Crawley and East Grinstead running under the number 424.

A supplementary service was provided over the Horley to Smallfield section especially to convey visitors to and from Smallfield Hospital. T 787 is seen on the shuttle service in Smallfield on 21st August 1954 having just passed a motor cycle combination heading in the other direction. This bus was one of five 15T13s which dated from 1948 to be transferred to Crawley Garage during the summer of 1953.

From 15th June 1949 a second supplementary service, also numbered 424, was provided from Smallfield to run to Horne. T 782 is seen at the Horne terminus on 6th September 1958. After the bus strike, falling passenger numbers meant that both of the shuttle services to Outwood and Horne ran for the last time on 27th October 1958. The crews must have been sorry to lose such easy duties running through pleasant countryside with so few passengers.

In the mid-1960s London Transport was considering new designs of buses which resulted in 50 Leyland Atlanteans being acquired for the Central Area and eight Daimler Fleetlines for use in the Country Area. The Fleetlines were chosen to work on route 424 and were all allocated to East Grinstead Garage. They took up their duties on 15th September 1965 and were finished in Lincoln green with a thick cream band between decks. A brand new XF 8 is seen at the Abergavenny Arms at Copthorne heading for Reigate on 26th September 1965.

The performance of the Atlanteans was proving disappointing so for comparison purposes, on 17th April 1966, the eight Fleetlines were transferred to Highgate Garage for use on route 271 and a similar number of Atlanteans were transferred to East Grinstead. Red-liveried XA 39 is seen in Reigate on 12th June 1966.

The Fleetlines returned to East Grinstead on 10th July 1966 and XF 5 is seen at Irons Bottom whilst heading for Reigate on 7th August. They were subsequently the subject of experimental operation when from 2nd October they were worked by just the driver at slack times with the top deck closed off as double-deck one-man operation was not legally permitted. Conventional working resumed on 2nd January 1967.

One of the most photographed routes in the Reigate area was the frying pan route 447. A frequent service starting at Redhill it ran via Doods Road, Reigate, Meadvale, Earlswood and Redhill to South Merstham. An additional section ran from Reigate to South Merstham via the same route and continued via Caterham to Woldingham. The route retained the 4Q4 type until March 1953 when the first Country Area RF buses to be delivered took over. Q 71 is seen at Reigate Red Cross on 28th July 1951. The destination blind shows the complicated nature of the route.

During 1953 and 1954 three light-weight single-deckers were trialled alongside the RFs on routes 447 and 711 from Reigate Garage and also on routes 208/A from Dalston Garage in the Central Area. The vehicles concerned were a Bristol LS5G, a Leyland Tiger Cub PSUC1/1 and an AEC Monocoach which was fitted with a 44-seat Park Royal body. The Monocoach was subsequently modified with "Monocontrol" transmission which was an alternative to the pre-selective gear box and returned to Reigate to work on route 447 from January 1956 until May 1957. The bus was registered NLP635 and never allocated a fleet number and is seen in Bell Street, Reigate on 25th May 1956.

Certain journeys avoided running via Meadvale by running directly between Redhill and Reigate via either Main Road (447A) or Blackborough Road (447B). RF 569 is seen at Woldingham Station running to Reigate Garage as a 447B on 8th May 1959, during the last week of crew operation to Woldingham.

RF 571 is seen returning from Woldingham between Caterham and Chaldon on 8th May 1959. From 13th May the section between Woldingham and Merstham was surrendered to route 440 which became one-man operated.

During 1959 some red RFs were temporarily allocated to Reigate to enable Country RFs to be converted for one-man duties. RF 509 is seen in Earlsbrook Road, Earlswood on 8th May 1959 heading for Redhill via Meadvale and Reigate. The bus returned to the Central Area in October 1960.

In 1953 much of the South Merstham service was extended to serve the new London County Council estate at Merstham. With the conversion of all of the Country Area RFs to one-man operation being completed in 1959 Green Line RFs were used on the remaining crew-operated routes. RF 168 is seen at the setting-down point in Merstham Delabole Road on 30th March 1963. The busy route was finally converted to one-man operation on the last day of 1966.

Following the local authority lowering the road surface at a railway bridge in 1954 one RLH was drafted onto the route to work the section between Redhill and Delabole Road for schools traffic and at other busy times. RLH 27 is seen on route 447B heading for Delabole Road passing the Jolly Brickmakers in Frenches Road, Holmethorpe on 25th May 1967. The RLH operation lasted until December 1967.

Route 439 linking Reigate with Dorking via Brockham was converted to one-man operation in October 1965 when it absorbed Dorking local route 429 to become a frying pan style route with projections to South Holmwood and Newdigate. Red RF 438 was loaned to the Country Area during 1967 and early 1968 and is seen taking on passengers at Redhill Station prior to departure on its complicated journey on 25th September 1967. The destination blind is noteworthy.

Route 439A was just one morning peak hour journey in both directions from Reigate to Merstham via Wray Common. The parent route 439 ran to Redhill via Wray Common. The 439A was converted to one-man operation in May 1959. RF 670 is seen in Nutfield Road, South Merstham returning to Reigate Garage on 23rd May 1966. The route was withdrawn upon the conversion of the 447 group to one-man operation on 31st December 1966 being covered by new route 447C.

New route 447C ran from Merstham, Delabole Road to Merstham Feathers via Redhill, Earlswood, Reigate and Wray Common. Former Green Line RF 270 stands at the picking-up point at Delabole Road on the route on 22nd June 1967. The bus stop and rural type shelter complete with its enamel-iron sign complete the scene.

Route 440 was a short route linking Redhill and Salfords with companion route 440A performing an even shorter run between Redhill and Redstone Estate. Q 12 is seen standing outside Lakers Hotel at Redhill Station on 28th July 1951.

In May 1959 routes 440 and 440A were converted to one-man working and extended from Redhill to Woldingham replacing a section of route 447. RF 574 is seen at the Woldingham, The Ridge terminus on 28th October 1961 before departure to Redstone Estate on route 440A. The driver has switched on the interior lights.

RF 561 is performing a short journey over the Redhill to Salfords section and was captured in Honeycrock Lane, Salfords on 30th June 1961. The Monotype Factory at Salfords was employed on essential war work and in 1942 it was a condition that only grey-painted 4Q4s were allowed to run to this seemingly delightful spot.

Route 430 was RT-worked linking Reigate and Redhill via South Park and Redhill General Hospital. From 1st January 1967 it was converted to one-man RFs on Sundays when it was extended from Redhill to Merstham, Delabole Road replacing a section of route 447 on that day. RF 584 was photographed on Portland Drive, South Merstham on 12th March 1967. The lower-case blind display is set out in an appalling fashion. London Transport obviously felt that their passengers' eye sight was of a very high standard!

The very first Country Area conventional one-man operated **MB** class buses entered service on **9th March 1968** perhaps unsurprisingly from Reigate Garage on local route 447. Drivers and passengers were still on a learning curve when this photograph was taken of **MB 85** on the second day of service in Pendleton Road near the junction with Somerset Road. The bus has a low driving position which did not prove popular with drivers

Route 430 was the first to be converted to **MBS** Autofare operation on 23rd November 1968. The immense length of these vehicles made it difficult for the drivers to negotiate them through narrow roads in housing estates and passengers strongly objected to the minimal amount of seating provided. Eventually seven additional single seats were fitted in the standing area on these buses. MBS 274 is seen in South Park, Reigate on 1st March 1969 and has a high driving position.

Route 405 was the main route linking Croydon to Crawley and, at one time, Horsham. RT 613 heading for Crawley gives parked vehicles a wide berth in Woodlands Road, Earlswood on 29th August 1970. The bus has been fitted with a side via blind in the front box.

One of the last economies under London Transport in October 1969 was the conversion of a number of double-deck routes to one-man operation on Sundays. Route 405 was so treated with RF 623 seen at Lowfield Heath on 12th April 1970.

Green Line route 711 linked Reigate with central London and High Wycombe and was converted to one-man operation on 23rd November 1968. Refurbished RF 93 is seen in Banstead High Street heading for High Wycombe on 3rd May 1970. Despite five months of London Country's ownership the coach still shows the London Transport bullseye.

Route 426 was a long-established Crawley circular linking the town with Tinsley Green, Horley, Charlwood and Ifield with origins going back to East Surrey days. RF 592 is seen performing the clock-wise circuit south of Horley in Balcombe Road at Burstow Hall Corner on 18th May 1963.

To help meet the needs of the developing Crawley NewTown a supplementary service was provided on route 426 between Ifield and Three Bridges Station on 13th June 1951. T 679, displaced from Green Line duties, is seen working on the shuttle service on 5th September 1953 in Three Bridges Road.

The 426 shuttle service was subsequently converted to RT operation in October 1953 and renumbered 426A on 11th August 1954. As the new town expanded it gained extensions at both ends of the route. In this view taken on 26th July 1963 RT 990 is seen at the Ifield Station terminus in Ifield Drive waiting to work the next journey to Pound Hill.

The short route 483 running from Crawley to Northgate was introduced on 6th May 1953 being worked by one STL. Open fields were a backdrop to the Northgate terminus when this photograph of STL 1705 was taken on 5th September 1953. This bus was taken out of stock in November that year but Crawley Garage retained STLs until 11th August 1954. The route was withdrawn in January 1958 when the section to Northgate was handed over to Southdown Motor Services.

Route 476 commenced on 19th May 1954 running between Crawley and Langley Green. RT 3676 stands at the Langley Green terminus just three months after the route's introduction on 21st August. With new services of this nature the initial terminal arrangements were often temporary pending further building and fixed stop posts were not always provided. Houses under construction can be seen in the background.

Route 476 was extended across Crawley town centre to Tilgate and Furnace Green as these areas developed and loop working without stand time was introduced. RT 4765 was captured by the camera in Weald Drive, approaching Tilgate on 30th October 1966.

Route 405B was introduced in 1961 to link Redhill and Gatwick with the Crawley industrial area, town centre and Tilgate during peak hours. RT 4777 pulls away from a stop in Fleming Way whilst heading for Tilgate on 3rd June 1966. Note industrial units under construction in the background.

Works route 476B linked the Manor Royal industrial area with Furnace Green having been introduced on 17th July 1963. RT 3636 is just about to reverse while performing the terminal working at an undeveloped Furnace Green on 26th July 1965. Note that concrete blocks have been placed in the unmade-up road to prevent its use other than for reversing. Route 476B was absorbed into the 405B at the end of 1966.

Route 851 was a Sunday afternoon hospital service linking Three Bridges and Crawley with Smallfield Hospital introduced in May 1954 and withdrawn after 3rd October 1965. RT 1059 conveys a handful of passengers back from the hospital on 26th September 1965 and has just turned from Three Bridges Road into Mitchells Road.

The 853 group of routes had been introduced in 1955 and 1958 to link the industrial area with other parts of the new town. RT 3653 is in Manor Royal near Newton Road bound for Crawley town centre on 22nd June 1967. The bus advertises the new Green Line route, 727, linking Crawley and Luton which had been introduced in the previous month.

RT 4498 has just entered Worth Road when heading for the Pound Hill South terminus on 22nd June 1967. The via blind showing Works Journey is of interest. The use of route numbers in the 850 series came to an end when, after 1st December 1967, the 853 group workings were covered by the 405B and 476A.

Originally worked by Sargents of East Grinstead Ltd. which sold out to Southdown Motor Services works routes between East Grinstead and Crawley were passed to London Transport on 30th April 1951. As Crawley developed, the 438 group acquired suffixes A to C due to combinations of intermediate route variations. RT 4745 heading for Crawley on route 438C is seen near the old Gatwick Airport Station on 1st August 1966. Part of the service was one-man operated and RF 226 is seen at the same location running as route 438 to Crawley. The two journeys ran just a few minutes apart and neither seems very busy for works services travelling with the peak flow.

The 438 group services were revised from 2nd January 1967 when a number of additional journeys were provided as a replacement for the section of the branch line between Three Bridges and East Grinstead. The former 424 when working journeys were renumbered 438A running from East Grinstead to Crawley via Crawley Down, Copthorne and Three Bridges. RT 3636 is seen near Crawley Down working a journey from East Grinstead to Three Bridges on 11th September 1970.

RT 3044 is seen at Crawley Bus Station awaiting a fresh crew on 16th May 1965 en route from West Croydon to Horsham. The destination blind shows 'via Crawley' to differentiate it from the 414 which ran from West Croydon to Horsham via Dorking

The section of route between Crawley and Horsham had a complicated history being served by routes 434 and 473 until January 1957 when passenger demand was such that double-deck route 405 was extended from Crawley to Horsham. Declining passenger numbers reversed the position from 15th March 1969 which saw the 434 and 473 replacing the 405 over this section. From this date three MB types were allocated together with the existing RFs and RTs. MB 113 is seen at Marsh Green on 7th June 1969 whilst working from Edenbridge to Horsham on route 434.

When the 33 Country Area conventional one-man MB buses were allocated in the winter of 1968/9 they were spread very thinly across the network. Two Central Area buses MB 379 and 380 were allocated to Crawley to work alongside MB 113. This photograph shows MB 379 nearing the end of its journey in Kings Road, Horsham on 6th April 1969. Unlike their green cousins the red MB buses did not have a centre exit door.

A much more frequent service using double-deck buses was run between Horsham and Roffey Corner. This view shows Weymann-bodied front entrance STL 1470 working on the shuttle service also in Kings Road on 25th August 1951. The bus has been fitted with the wrong type of destination blind for the narrow aperture box. STL 1470 was new to Dorking Garage in November 1936 and after withdrawal in November 1951 was converted to tree lopper 971J and survives in preservation.

An alternative service between Horsham and Roffey Corner via Littlehaven to the north of the Crawley Road had been provided by Hants & Sussex Motor Services Ltd. which ceased operating in December 1954 having been placed into receivership. In May 1955 London Transport took over the route as 434A and from January 1957 it was renumbered 405A. RT 4755 is seen on route 405A at the junction of Kings Road and Rusper Road on 11th July 1959.

When the 434 was reinstated to Horsham in 1969 the entire service was routed via Littlehaven. Despite the introduction of the MB type on the route an RT was still employed on the Horsham short journeys. RT 4554 is seen at Roffey Corner on 7th June 1969 displaying a side via blind in the front box.

From October 1963 certain journeys on route 405A were projected through to Redhill and West Croydon due to headway reductions on route 405. RT 3676 is seen at Horsham Station on 16th May 1965 where the driver has yet to change the destination blind for the return journey. Behind is RT 4536 on the slightly longer route 414 to West Croydon via Dorking.

RT 4536, the second bus in the above photograph, waits on the stand at Horsham Station for departure time to West Croydon. Route 414 offered a more scenic route by running via Dorking and Reigate. The destination West Croydon via Wellesley Road dates from the opening of West Croydon Bus Station on 31st July 1963 when northbound buses were so routed instead of running via North End in both directions

With the failure of Hants & Sussex Motor Services Ltd., London Transport stepped in and introduced route 852 from Three Bridges to Ewhurst via Crawley, Faygate, Horsham and Oakwood Hill on 21st December 1954. Following some adverse comments from within the bus industry for operating outside of its designated boundary to the north-west of Horsham, London Transport withdrew after 17th May 1955, retaining just the Three Bridges to Horsham section. GS 82 heading for Ewhurst was photographed to the west of Wallis Wood when the route had just four days left to run over this section.

Red RTs were often temporarily loaned to the Country Area to help out at busy times especially when green RTs were required for Green Line duplication. Red RT 4278 is seen at the stand at South Holmwood, Holly & Laurel on August Bank Holiday Monday, 4th August 1958, bound for West Croydon on route 414. Just the essential blinds have been fitted at the front for route identification.

Route 449 was introduced in March 1950 linking Dorking with Ewhurst. It subsequently gained extensions to Goodwyns Farm Estate and South Holmwood with the lengthy section to Ewhurst being withdrawn in October 1958. C 77, the first of the Central Area batch with Weymann bodywork, stands at Dorking Bus Station on 20th October 1951 prior to working a short journey to Chart Downs Estate. Like a number of the class the bus has had its front bumper removed.

RT 3461 working between Goodwyns Farm Estate and Chart Downs Estate is seen at the latter terminus on 26th July 1963. The route was RF worked on Sundays and in 1969 lost its RT in favour of MB 82, the only one allocated to Dorking at the time.

The lengthy route 470 from Warlingham and Chelsham terminated at Dorking Bus Station. Leatherhead's roof box RT 1064 forms the next departure to Warlingham on 11th July 1959. Although the route terminated here it was not worked by Dorking Garage. All of the roof box-bodied RTs had been withdrawn from the Country Area by January 1964.

RT 3116 makes for a fine sight when seen in Ewell Road, Cheam on 23rd August 1969. Much of the length of route 470 was in Central bus territory with only the extremities being true Country Area. The intermediate points blind has become a little awry due to the use of inferior quality linen backing.

Route 433 was a rural route linking Ranmore and Coldharbour via Dorking and was always poplar in the summer with ramblers going to the Surrey hills. Country Area C 45 with a body by Short Brothers of Rochester stands at the remote Dog Kennel Green terminus at Ranmore on 20th October 1951.

Route 429 formed a rather complicated circular from Dorking to Holmwood, Newdigate and Brockham back to Dorking with much of the service being fragmented. RT 3525 is seen approaching the terminus at Newdigate having come from Dorking via Brockham on 1st August 1958. Upon arrival here some buses then continued as route 439 via Holmwood and Dorking to Redhill.

The days of C 8 were numbered when seen in **Coldharbour** on 29th September 1953. When East Surrey had introduced this route in 1930 the intention had been to run beyond Coldharbour to Leith Hill but the state of the road over this section rendered it unsuitable for buses.

On 3rd October 1965 route 439 was converted to one-man operation and revised to absorb the former 429 journeys, that route being withdrawn. In addition to the through service from Redhill a number of short journeys were provided across Dorking. RF 249 was photographed at Strood Green on a run to South Holmwood on 5th June 1966.

Route 412 linked Dorking with the village of Sutton Abinger which was always referred to on the blinds as Holmbury St. Mary (Sutton) to avoid confusion with Sutton on the route 470. Throughout London Transport's tenure of operation an out-station was maintained at Holmbury St. Mary to save unproductive mileage with early and late buses running from and returning to Dorking. RF 605 was photographed on 17th July 1959 between Holmbury St. Mary and Sutton Abinger.

During the second half of 1951 a batch of 37 of the 10T10 class were overhauled and repainted into red livery for use in the Central Area where they would replace older members of the T class. Upon overhaul, however, some buses were temporarily returned to the Country Area. T 475 lays over between trips on route 412 at Dorking North Station on 20th October 1951. One of the alterations made was the provision of a route number holder above the sliding door. When these buses were used in the Central Area Metropolitan Police regulations required the entrance door to be secured in the open position at all times.

The TF class was of a revolutionary design, incorporating for the first time an underfloor engine, which was developed by London Transport and Leyland Motors with a prototype vehicle being delivered in 1937. The production batch of 12 private hire coaches and 75 Green Line coaches followed in 1939. Post-war the Green Line vehicles were to be found initially on routes 712, 713, 714, 723 and 727 and later also on 720 and 723A. TF 81 is seen at Eccleston Bridge, Victoria heading for Dorking on route 713 on 4th March 1951.

Dorking Garage was opened by London General Country Services on 16th March 1932 and incorporated a bus station frontage. RF 91 on route 712 stands by the coach compulsory stop on 21st June 1964. The route had normally run to Luton but from 25th October 1961 the service beyond St. Albans was reduced to Monday to Friday peak hours and Saturdays.

Route 425 linked Dorking with Guildford running through some very pleasant Surrey countryside and was popular with day-trippers and later Green Rover riders. Crew-operated RF 694 heads for Dorking North Station at Gomshall on 10th September 1955. The route was not converted to one-man operation until October 1958.

RT 3043 is on the lengthy route 408 which had its southern terminus at Guildford. Having been in the suburbs between Chelsham and Epsom the bus is now in the countryside at East Horsley on 5th September 1959. Two cars have caught up with the bus but the general absence of other traffic is noteworthy and typical of the period.

At Gomshall the 425 was briefly joined by the 448 which ran into Guildford via Newlands Corner, a popular Surrey beauty spot. GS 35 was photographed in Peaslake on 19th July 1964. The route was run jointly with Tillingbourne Valley Motor Services Ltd. between Guildford and Peaslake with some London Transport journeys continuing to Ewhurst.

Route 448A was just a short Guildford town route running to Pewley Way, using buses off route 448, which had been introduced in August 1950. GS 25 is seen at Pewley Way on 18th August 1962. The report of the Phelps Brown Committee of Enquiry published in February 1964 contained a recommendation that, where possible, uneconomic routes should be handed over to private operators. Accordingly routes 448 and 448A ran for the last time on 11th August 1964 after which Tillingbourne Valley assumed full responsibility for both routes.

Guildford local route 408A ran from the Bushy Hill area of Merrow into the town centre. RT 3137 makes the right turn from Bushy Hill Drive into Epsom Road while heading for Onslow Street Bus Station on 18th August 1962. The style of the lazy blind is interesting.

Route 432 indirectly linked Great Bookham with Guildford by running via Effingham Junction and West Horsley and had been converted to one-man operation in October 1957. RF 652 is seen in Church Road near Bookham Station heading for Guildford on 17th July 1959. This bus was withdrawn in 1972 and sold to the Ipswich Coach Company.

Both Addlestone and Guildford garages operated the RLH class on various routes in the south-west corner of the network. The 463 from Walton to Guildford took a longer route than its companion route 436 by running via West Clandon and Merrow instead of the Portsmouth Road direct. RLH 26 passes Clandon Station on its way to Guildford on 19th July 1964. This was one of the members of its class that survived into London Country ownership.

One of the first batch of the RLH class dating from 1950 was RLH 16 which was allocated to Godstone until 1962 when it was transferred to Addlestone. In this view taken on Christmas Eve 1965 the bus is seen on route 463 at Send. RLH 16 was withdrawn the following month and passed to Elkes Biscuits of Uttoxeter.

Green Line route 715 was noted for operating the 6Q6 class from June 1946 until the arrival of the new RF coaches in 1952. A somewhat weary-looking Q 221 is seen in Guildford Garage where an RT on Green Line relief duties may be seen in the background on 9th June 1951. Q 221 was new in December 1936 and once displaced from Green Line work was used as a bus until withdrawal in April 1953.

103

Route 415 provided a service along the Portsmouth Road from Guildford to Ripley where connections could be made to Central Area bus route 215. Dwindling passenger numbers saw it reduced to mostly just short journeys between Guildford and Burpham. In this view taken on 18th August 1962 RT 4755 is seen at Burpham heading for Guildford.

The 436 provided a trunk route between Staines and Guildford with alternate journeys from Staines running instead to Ripley as 436A. In this delightful rural scene RLH 21 pulls away from the stop at Send Common whilst bound for Ripley on 2nd August 1965. Twenty members of the RLH class entered service during 1950 being originally intended for Midland General. RLH 21 was the first of a batch of 56 buses to be specifically ordered by London Transport for delivery during late 1952.

Route 418 provided a service from Bookham Station to Kingston via a rather more indirect routeing than the 406 which it met at Epsom. On 17th July 1959 RT 650 was recorded near Bookham Station heading for Kingston.

RT 3173 stands at Bookham Station on 22nd July 1967. A loop working was performed at Bookham Station with some journeys departing via Preston Cross. The route number 418A applied to a few journeys which ran directly via the main road at Ashtead rather than via Ashtead Station. The double-depth slip board specifies the minimum fares which applied on leaving Kingston, an initiative to deter short riders to the exclusion of others.

Route 468 linked Chessington Zoo with Epsom and had some southwards projections to Leatherhead and Effingham. RT 986 was photographed at West Ewell, Bungalow Stores on 28th December 1965. During very cold weather newspaper was sometimes fixed to the radiator grill to prevent an excessive intake of cold air.

Although not on line of route of the 406 and 406A Leatherhead Garage put out the majority of the buses, supplemented by Reigate. Running from Kingston to Redhill, route 406 was an obvious choice for Green Rover travellers. RT 3133 is seen in Epsom Lane North approaching Tadworth while working from Kingston to Redhill on 8th August 1959.

Certain journeys ran as 406A to serve housing in Merland Rise instead of direct via Epsom Lane North. In addition during Monday to Friday peak periods a few journeys ran Express between Epsom and Kingston, displaying white on blue blinds. RT 2982 was photographed in a busy Epsom High Street on 7th June 1967. The only short working to Epsom on the express route was the 08.52 from Kingston.

Epsom is, of course, famous for its racecourse which involved special services being provided at times of race meetings. RT 2499 works special route 406F on 7th June 1967 and will no doubt leave Epsom Station with a full load of hopeful punters for the course. Extra buses were drafted in from across the southern network, in this case the bus has come from East Grinstead Garage.

107

A very smartly turned out RT 3729 is seen heading for Kingston at Tattenham Corner Grandstand on 1st September 1972 before London Country has let standards slip. Note the wooden shelter incorporating an enamel-iron bus stop sign. The bus was withdrawn from service a matter of just six weeks later.

A special hospital service was run between Leatherhead and Netherne Hospital at Hooley on Wednesday and Sunday afternoons. RT 4631 is seen on route 472 near Netherne Hospital on 7th October 1962. As the blind suggests, only a limited number of stops were provided and in addition passengers were only conveyed to and from the hospital.

Epsom local route 419 achieved notoriety in March 1953 when it became the first route to be worked by one-man operated RF buses. The experiment was successful and the rest, as they say, is history. In this view RF 637 is loading up in Epsom High Street whilst working on the route on 22nd April 1967.

Another Epsom local route was the 481 which had been introduced on 6th May 1953 to link the Wells Estate with the town centre. Originally worked by 20-seaters CR 43 is seen in Wells Road on 26th September 1953. The CR class was a revolutionary design with a rear engine developed by London Transport and Leyland Motors and, apart from the prototype, were all delivered in 1939. Due to the Second World War they spent a number of years in store.

The GS class superseded the CR and C vehicles on route 481 later in 1953. GS 5 is also seen in Wells Road on 18th June 1955. Note the "Pay as you enter" sticker applied to the nearside windscreen. The GS class survived on the route until December 1967.

RF 583 was photographed on route 481 at **Well Way** in the heart of the estate on 9th August 1969. An RF took over from the GS in 1958 but as passenger numbers increased a GS was also allocated to the route between 1963 and 1967.

RTs made occasional trips on the 481 at busy times or through cross working. In this view at **The Wells** a very smartly turned out RT 4202 is seen conveying school children. The bus has the yellow London Country fleet name applied and the blinds are well presented. The picture was taken on 29th March 1973.

Route 416 provided a service between Leatherhead and Esher and at one time had been the haunt of the experimental Green Line coach RTC 1. RT 3733 is seen heading for Leatherhead at Oxshott Heath on 19th October 1957, shortly before the route was revised and converted to RF one-man operation.

When the 416 was converted to one-man operation it was extended to run from Esher to Tadworth Station and Boxhill absorbing route 435 which was withdrawn. RF 637 is seen leaving Esher in Copsem Lane heading for Boxhill on 11th March 1970.

Former Green Line 10T10, T 625 is seen arriving back in Leatherhead on route 422 from Boxhill on 20th October 1951. Route 422 had a minor deviation from route 416 in that it did not serve the R.A.F. Hospital at Headley Court. T 625 which is in the two-tone green livery was taken out of stock in November 1954.

The newer order on route 422 is represented by RF 636 which was captured at Boxhill, Greenacres terminus on 22nd June 1967. By this time in addition to the front "Pay as you enter" slip board a double-depth one with black lettering on yellow was provided in an attempt to encourage passengers to have their fare money ready. Route 422 had been introduced in June 1948 as one of the routes provided over previously unserved territory.

The 9T9 class was a batch of 50 vehicles built for Green Line service in 1936. They were not officially allocated to Green Line work after the war and served out their days on Country bus duties. T 449 in the white and green bus livery stands at Leatherhead Station prior to departing for Staines on the lengthy route 462 via Weybridge and Chertsey on 20th October 1951. The bus had less than five months' life ahead of it, being withdrawn in March 1952.

Route 462A was a special service running from Leatherhead to Leatherhead Court, a special hospital for disabled people in Woodlands Road. RF 695 waits at Leatherhead Station on 26th July 1963. A fine example of a railway banner type repeater signal may be seen immediately above the bus.

A low railway bridge between Staines and Chertsey and another at Woking Station meant that some routes in the Addlestone area required the use of low-height double-deckers. During the Second World War passenger demand increases meant that a number of former single-deck routes were worked by low-bridge buses, of which London Transport was desperately short. It was a case of make do and mend. ST 140 was delivered new to National in 1930 and is seen at Staines West Station before departure to Ripley on 29th August 1949.

ST 163 was one of a batch of six buses with AEC chassis and low-height bodies by Short Brothers delivered to National in 1930 for use on route N6 running from Watford to Berkhamsted via Amersham. The bus is seen in Addlestone on 31st August 1952 working on route 461A from Botleys Park to Walton.

ST 163 is seen again on 31st August 1952 in Weybridge whilst running from Staines to Walton. At that time the timetable was arranged so that the buses cross-worked between the two routes at Walton.

STL 2229 looking smartly turned out in the green and white livery lays over between trips at Staines West Station before leaving for Walton on route 461 on 25th June 1950. This bus was withdrawn in February 1953. The bus was soon to be transferred to Godstone following the allocation of eight RLHs to Addlestone.

STL 2311 previously seen working from Godstone on route 410 was transferred to Addlestone Garage and is seen at Woking Station on 24th September 1950. Route 436 which ran from Staines to Guildford had been curtailed at Woking on 1st June 1943 to concentrate the low-bridge buses on the busier section between Staines and Woking. A single-deck operated 436B covered the section on to Guildford.

The Godstone STLs were temporarily placed into store following the arrival of the first batch of the RLH class but were found to be in such good condition that they were sent to Addlestone to allow routes 436 and 436A to resume through running between Staines and Guildford and Ripley respectively. STL 1055 is seen standing on Addlestone Garage forecourt on 31st August 1952 with one of the eight RLHs from the original batch parked behind.

The RLH class was to become a familiar feature of the south-west corner of the network for a period of twenty years with the last examples running until the last day of July 1970. One bus which survived to the end was RLH 47 seen at Woodham, The Victoria on 29th July 1962.

One of the second batch of RLHs which entered service in November 1952 is seen passing under the offending low bridge in Chertsey Lane, Egham Hythe on 21st June 1967. RLH 50 is working between Staines and Ripley on route 436A.

RLH 35 is seen on the stand at Staines on 1st March 1969 prior to departure to Ripley on route 436A. Following the closure of Staines West Station in March 1965 the terminus was now described as Moor Lane. The bus advertises the popular Green Rover tickets which had been introduced in 1956 at a cost of five shillings. By this time the cost had risen to seven shillings which still represented very good value for a day out exploring the network.

Route 461 provided a link between Staines and Walton and while once a daily regular service by the end of London Transport's control it had been reduced to journeys running on Monday to Friday only. RLH 21 passes through Addlestone while heading for Walton on 3rd March 1965. This bus passed through of a number of different hands after being sold out of service in 1971 and was eventually exported to the United States in 1977.

Route 463 had been introduced in May 1946 running between Walton and Woking to strengthen the service on sections of routes 461 and 436/A. On 27th September 1950 it was extended from Woking to Guildford running via Merrow. RLH 14 is seen passing Oatlands Park between Walton and Weybridge heading for Guildford on 26th October 1967. The arrangement of the low-height body is such that the passenger in the upper deck front seat will not be enjoying the view but will be looking down on the road surface a few yards in front of the bus. RLH 14 spent its entire working life at Addlestone Garage from June 1950 until July 1970.

Route 461A from Walton to Botleys Park could be worked by normal double-deckers but RLHs were often seen on the route having cross-worked from route 461. RLH 48 stands at the Walton terminus on 14th May 1955.

Vast numbers of short journeys were provided on route 462 to convey workers to and from Vickers Works at Weybridge which is now the site of Brooklands Museum. Roof box STL 1749, in red livery, showing no route number stops in Weybridge town centre on 22nd May 1954 while taking home-going workers to Addlestone. The last STL buses were withdrawn from Addlestone Garage on 1st August 1954.

Addlestone's RTs were restricted to certain routes, Green Line duplication and special journeys from Vickers Works at Weybridge. RT 4783 is heading for St. Peters Hospital on route 461A while passing along Oatlands Drive on 26th October 1967. This bus was finally withdrawn from service at Harlow Garage in November 1975.

122

In 1965 the Vickers name gave way to British Aircraft Corporation. Correctly-blinded RT 3431 was photographed in Brooklands Road, Weybridge on 13th March 1969 on the short route 462B from BAC Works to Walton. The bus was sold to Tillingbourne Valley Services in March 1972.

Route 456B was worked by both RF and RT types from Addlestone via Weybridge, BAC Works, West Byfleet and Woodham. RF 667 is seen on 13th June 1969 in Parvis Road approaching West Byfleet Corner on one such journey. This RF was subsequently transferred to Amersham Garage from which it was withdrawn in January 1976.

Route 474 was a Monday to Friday shoppers' service introduced on 1st November 1965 linking Addlestone with Botleys Park where it performed a large loop working through some previously unserved roads. A smartly turned out RF 666 was captured in Green Lane on 13th June 1969, the last day of service, the route being withdrawn through a lack of patronage.

Routes 427, 437 and 456 were single-deck worked routes running Weybridge - West Byfleet - Woking with various intermediate variations of route. Former Green Line 10T10, T 516 is seen running through a rather rural Byfleet bound for Woking on 24th May 1953. T 516 was taken out of stock on 1st January 1954.

RF 676 was photographed in Parvis Road, approaching West Byfleet Corner on 13th June 1969 heading for Woking on route 437. The 427 and 437 both ran via Byfleet but the 437 ran direct via Woking Road whereas the 427 and 456 deviated to serve Pyrford Schools.

London Transport was keen to experiment with one-man operated vehicles fitted with separate entrance and exit doors which was seen as a means of reducing stop dwell times. In 1960 a batch of AEC Reliances with Willowbrook bodywork was being supplied to Grimsby-Cleethorpes Transport and London Transport acquired three buses as an extension of the production run. They were tried on a number of the busier one-man operated routes and between January and June 1961 came to Addlestone for use on the 427/437/456 group. RW 2 arrives back in Addlestone on route 427 from Woking on 2nd April 1961.

T 636 was photographed in a somewhat deserted Addlestone on Sunday 24th May 1953. A large Union Jack flag is to be seen directly above the bus and has been flown as part of the Coronation celebrations soon to take place. The 456 ran via Woodham instead of Byfleet and in a second view taken on the same day the bus is passing through New Haw.

The group of routes had been converted to one-man operation in October 1958 and over the years the service was gradually reduced, especially on Sundays. RF 674 heading for Addlestone on route 456 is seen at Pyrford Schools. There was an unfulfilled proposal that these routes would have been operated by the first Merlins in the Country Area from 29th May 1966.

Odd RT workings could be found on routes 427, 437 and 456 for school and works requirements. RT 4553 is seen in East Hill at Maybury and is just about to turn into Linkway to reverse on 29th February 1972. The bus will no doubt return with a full load of school children. RT 4553 is on loan from Windsor to Addlestone and under London Country standards have been allowed to slip with the bus showing signs of roof damage caused by unpruned trees. Despite over two years of London Country control the destination still refers to Addlestone L.T. Garage!

RT 4752 makes for a splendid view running through Sheerwater on its way to Woking on 18th August 1962. Route 420 linked Woking with West Byfleet and was worked by both the RT and RLH classes. Note the alternately painted black and white kerbstones in the background.

Route 717 was introduced in May 1946 linking Woking and Welwyn Garden City. In October 1955 it was revised to run between Victoria and Welwyn Garden City with a new route 716A running between Woking and Stevenage. Shortly before this alteration the driver of RF 142 pulls out in Woodham to overtake a lady cyclist on 10th September 1955. The RF entered service new to Addlestone in February 1952.

CRL 4 was a prototype Routemaster fitted with an Eastern Coach Works body for Green Line work and unlike the other three Routemaster prototype vehicles was used in passenger service right up until 1979. Tried on various routes it was sent to Stevenage in December 1960 for a spell on routes 716 and 716A. The unique vehicle is seen waiting for a fresh crew at Addlestone Garage on 29th July 1962 while en route from Chertsey to Hitchin.

Routemaster coaches were newly allocated to the routes serving the new towns including the 716 and 716A. Their appearance changed over the years with the modified front air intake grill between the decks and after overhaul the removal of the between-decks metal bullseye in favour of a forward transfer. RMC 1491 is seen running through Sheerwater Estate nearing the end of its long journey to Woking on 13th June 1969.

Route 441D had at one time been a regular service between Staines and Virginia Water but after the 1956 summer season it was reduced to provide school journeys only leaving the Green Line and Aldershot & District service 1 from Egham to provide a regular service. The morning journey to Virginia Water ran via St. Jude's Road, Victoria Street and Harvest Road in Englefield Green presumably so that school children did not have to cross the busy A30 to reach a bus stop. RT 2539 is the only bus of the day to run along Victoria Street, Englefield Green on 9th September 1970.

Route 441C ran between Staines and Englefield Green, Larchwood Drive which was not served by the through route 441. RT 3203 is seen in Kingsley Avenue just after leaving the Larchwood Drive terminus on 10th February 1962. Staines Central Station was the former Southern Railway station and is today the only railway station in the town.

The Egham Motor Company which was acquired by the Board in February 1934 had run two rural routes between Staines and Virginia Water via Stroude or Thorpe which became 466 and 469 respectively. The terminus was a loop working which was just outside the London Passenger Transport Area and had to be abandoned later in 1934 leaving Knowle Hill unserved. Under the 1947 legislation London Transport was again able to run to Knowle Hill with the 466 being extended from Virginia Water in May 1950. RF 598 stands at Knowle Hill terminus on 1st June 1959 shortly after partial conversion of the route to one-man operation.

RT 3397 stands at Staines West Station on 21st March 1964 prior to working a short journey to Thorpe on route 469. Worked by Leyland Cubs before the Second World War the route was converted to double-deck operation in 1943 due to increased passenger demand. This RT did not make it into London Country ownership being withdrawn in July 1969.

Passenger numbers did not remain constant on route 469 and in two phases during 1964 and 1965 the fall in demand allowed conversion to one-man operation. Former Green Line RF 197 heads through Thorpe Green on 11th March 1967 on its way to Virginia Water.

133

Route 493 was a special hospital service between Englefield Green and St. Peters Hospital at Botleys Park consisting of one return journey on Wednesday and Sunday afternoons. RT 3211 is passing through Stroude on 29th July 1962. The route was withdrawn in May 1965 with the number 493 subsequently being allocated to the Orpington local service, formerly 854.

Following the Wilson government's decision - Dr. Beeching merely made recommendations - that the West Drayton to Staines branch should close, Central buses provided a replacement service 225 but it could not serve Stanwell Moor, near Poyle Halt. This was overcome by the introduction of route 444 from 30th March 1965 on Tuesdays (later changed to Wednesdays) and Saturdays. A very smart RT 3508 is seen at Stanwell Moor on 3rd April, the second day of service. This bus was sold to Tillingbourne Valley Services in March 1972.

Racing at Ascot put a vast strain on resources with buses being borrowed from other garages as necessary. Special service 443 provided journeys between Staines and Ascot on race days. RT 3335 crosses Staines Bridge with a load of hopeful punters bound for Ascot on 21st June 1967. The bus has been drafted in from Amersham for the race period.

In addition to route 443 vast numbers of duplicates were provided on Green Line route 701 at times of race meetings, with most starting from Victoria plus some working right through from Gravesend. RT 4043 is seen at Blacknest between Virginia Water and Ascot with a full load of passengers on 21st June 1967. The bus is on loan from Harlow Garage.

The main trunk route out of Staines to the north was the 441 running to High Wycombe or Hedgerley Village. RT 3616 devoid of advertisements is seen on 16th December 1967 joining the main route at Hedgerley Corner having started at Hedgerley Village. The destination blind reflects the renaming of the Southern Region station after the branch line to Staines West had closed. This RT was also sold to Tillingbourne Valley Services in March 1972.

Route 460 linked Staines with Slough via Datchet and as a result of headway reductions on route 441 was projected on Sundays from Slough to Hedgerley Village from October 1963 until November 1964. RT 3200 approaches Hedgerley Corner bound for Hedgerley Village on 19th July 1964.

Falling passenger numbers saw route 460 converted to one-man operation on the last day of 1966. RF 604 is seen passing Datchet Church on 22nd June 1967 working a short journey over the Slough to Datchet section of the route.

In addition to the main service on route 441 a number of short journeys were provided in the Slough area. RT 2157 stands outside Slough Station on 9th May 1965 having worked one such journey. The 'via Slough' intermediate points blind display was typical of such short workings.

Route 441B had been introduced during 1943 and for many years consisted of just one morning peak hour journey from Beaconsfield to Langley Village with no return working. RT 4173 is seen in Slough, Langley Road, near the site of the former London Transport bus garage which had been closed in 1937, whilst heading for Langley Village on 4th July 1967.

Routes 457 and 457A linked Windsor with Uxbridge and were popular with passengers on Summer Sundays when many extra buses were provided. For a number of years it was possible for Underground passengers to book through to Windsor on Sundays by changing to the buses at Uxbridge. RT 4100 heads for Uxbridge through Iver Heath on 4th July 1967.

Route 457A varied from the 457 by running via Upton Lea instead of direct via Uxbridge Road. RT 4768 stands in St. Albans Street at Windsor Castle on 9th August 1958. The bus behind would appear to be on the ill-fated route 444, shortly to be withdrawn.

Works journeys were run to Pinewood Film Studios at Iver Heath from Uxbridge as 457C and Windsor as 457D. RT 2157 was captured by the camera at Pinewood Studios on 26th August 1966. Note that the canopy blind shows route 400 – this often happened as a result of inter-working between routes.

Windsor Garage received a batch of ten RMLs in May 1966, nominally for use on the 446 and 484 group but with the complexities of cross-working they turned up on other routes. RML 2452 entered service new to Windsor in May 1966 and is seen on 16th June 1967 at Iver Heath heading for Uxbridge on route 457C.

Route 458 offered an alternative route between Slough and Uxbridge running via Langley and Cowley and was single-deck worked due to the low bridge at Langley Station. The route was very busy and retained conductors until November 1964. RF 541 passes the Memorial at Langley Village whilst heading for Slough on 9th May 1965.

Richings Park Estate at Iver had been servred by Central Area route 220 until September 1939 when it lost its service as a wartime economy measure. It remained unserved until July 1950 when route 459 was provided running from Uxbridge. RF 592 is seen standing at the Tower Arms terminus at Richings Park on 9th August 1958.

How the mighty are fallen! The once-busy route 457A was converted to RF one-man operation on Sundays as an economy measure in June 1969. RF 572 is seen crossing the canal bridge in Rockingham Road, Uxbridge on 19th October 1969.

Route 445 was acquired from the Borough Bus Service in 1935 and linked Windsor with Datchet. Over the years the route had been worked by small one-man operated buses, large single-deckers and even double-deck types. By the time that RF 542 was seen in Eton Road, Datchet on 18th February 1967, the service level had been very considerably reduced.

The origins of route 442 running between Slough and Farnham Royal via Stoke Poges went back to operation by the Great Western Railway. Under London Transport the route gained a summer season extension to Burnham Beeches in 1949. STL 994, one of a batch of 85 buses delivered in 1935 for the Country Area with front entrance Chiswick built bodies, stands at Slough Station on 14th May 1951 shortly before withdrawal.

The order for the GS buses was increased from 70 to 84 so as to permit the conversion of some under used crew-operated routes to one-man working. Incredibly RT-worked 442 was one such candidate receiving the GS class in 1954. GS 78 heading for Windsor is seen in Elliman Avenue, Slough on 9th August 1958. By this time the route had been reduced to four Monday to Friday journeys and just two on Saturdays and it was withdrawn in October 1958.

Route 474 had been introduced on Summer Sundays in 1948 running between Slough Station and Burnham Beeches via Farnham Road. Front entrance STL 1040 is seen in Slough, Bath Road on 6th August 1951. The route was withdrawn immediately after the bus strike in 1958.

Route 417 ran between Windsor and Langley Village via Slough and Langley Road with projections to Colnbrook at one end of the route and Old Windsor at the other. Red STL 489 stands outside Windsor Garage on 6th August 1951. The bus was new to Chalk Farm Garage in July 1934 and was taken out of stock in November 1953.

STL 974 is seen outside Windsor Garage between trips on route 417 on Bank Holiday Monday, 6th August 1951. One of the brand new RF private hire coaches in Lincoln green and grey livery stands behind. Windsor Garage would be extremely busy on Bank Holidays running vast numbers of duplicates and also hosting excursion and tours coaches. STL 974 was withdrawn later during the year.

RML 2309 pulls away from the stop in Langley Road at the junction of Middle Green Road bound for Windsor on route 417 on 22nd June 1967.

From 22nd January 1966 inroads were made with the troublesome London Transport boundary in Slough when an arrangement with Thames Valley saw new route 407 running from Langley Village to Cippenham and Thames Valley routes 60 and 69 from Maidenhead to Slough being extended eastwards to Langley Village. As a result the service on route 417 was considerably reduced. The driver of RT 603 climbs into the cab at Langley Village on 19th February 1966.

Some peak hour buses ran as 407A via Slough Trading Estate instead of a section of Bath Road as depicted by RT 4440 also seen at Langley Village. The uppercase and lowercase via blinds depicted in these two photographs make an interesting comparison. Note the rural type bus shelter in the background.

Routes 446 and 446A provided a frequent service between Slough and Farnham Road, The George with the 446 running via Whitby Road and the 446A via Manor Park. Buses usually returned from The George by the opposite route to which they had arrived which often resulted in the inappropriate route number being displayed. STL 504 in red livery stands at Slough Station between journeys on 6th August 1951 even though the routes had been officially converted to RT operation in June of that year.

A mud-spattered RT 3118 has just turned out of Northern Road into Stoke Poges Lane whilst returning to Slough on 8th February 1969 shortly before conversion to Autofare operation. Strictly speaking the route number should be 446A but the prominent via display in the ultimate destination box makes the routeing very clear.

148

Primarily due to severe staff shortage at Windsor Garage a number of the Slough local routes were converted to MBS Autofare operation on 15th March 1969. By this time routes 446 and 446A have acquired a cross-town extension to serve Wexham Park Hospital where MBS 408 was photographed just after the conversion on 22nd March.

Route 446B linked Windsor and Slough with the extensive Slough Trading Estate which was located to the west of the town. RT 4734 pulls away from a request stop in Bath Road on an inclement 15th April 1966. The lazy display in the via blind box applies to routes 446 and 446A and the conductor has made some attempt to turn the blind down to obscure Farnham Road.

Route 444 provided additional facilities on Saturdays over routes 446 and 446A. Roof box RT 1018 stands in Mackenzie Street at Slough Station on 9th August 1958. The route was withdrawn later in the year in October. The stops in the area are numbered as part of the "Where to board your bus" publicity scheme. The stop carries E-Plates for routes 442, 444, 446 and 446A and the interesting Q plate reads "Elliman Avenue Northbound" and would no doubt fetch a very considerable sum today in auction! This bus survived on training duties until 1981 and was subsequently preserved.

Route 457B was a spare number which was allocated to a new route on 18th April 1956 running from Slough to serve new but rather drab housing at Wexham Court Farm Estate which was situated between Wexham Road and Uxbridge Road. RT 3809 is seen in the estate at the junction of The Frith and Knolton Way on 27th June 1959.

On 11th December 1957 routes 484/A/B running from Langley, Datchet and Colnbrook to Farnham Road gained extensions to serve new housing at Britwell. It was a joint venture with Thames Valley which ran route 64 to Britwell. RT 4770 is running through Readings Lane in Britwell on 27th June 1959. This bus was subsequently painted red and survived for another twenty years before being withdrawn as a trainer.

On 8th July 1959 route 457B and the 484 group projections to Britwell were replaced by new route 400 which was operated as a vast circular with stand time being allowed only at Britwell. RT 1012 is seen running in Readings Lane, Britwell on 2nd August 1965.

RT 4173 stands at Langley Village, The Harrow before returning to Windsor on route 484 via Bath Road and Slough on 22nd June 1967. The conductor has correctly set up the 'via Slough' display for the journey back to the garage.

RML buses were allocated to the 484 group in 1966 and RML 2455 is seen on route 484 at the Colnbrook, The Plough terminus on 1st August of that year. The RMLs were displaced from the routes by the Merlins in March 1969. RML 2455 was sold back to London Transport in 1978 and survives in preservation today.

The 484 group was converted to Autofare MBS operation on 15th March 1969. MBS 411 stands at Langley Village before running across Slough to Farnham Road. The MBS class was not popular with passengers due to the unreliability of the ticket issuing machines and the lack of seating and evidence showed that passengers preferred to use conventional buses where such services were available.

The 484 group did not run on Sundays and initially the 400 did not run to Britwell on Sundays so between May 1959 and November 1964 the Sunday service to Britwell was provided by route 441A running from Windsor Castle. RT 3735 stands at the Wentworth Avenue terminus in Britwell on 21st October 1962. As the route required just one bus not all buses in the garage would have had the blinds amended to show 441A so the Windsor engineering staff have produced a slip board showing the route number. Local children find the concrete bus shelter of interest!

Windsor Bridge was inspected by engineers on 10th April 1970 and the condition of the structure was so poor that it was closed to road traffic later that day. This involved a lengthy diversion via the relief road and Elizabeth Bridge and left Eton, which had been served by up to 20 buses per hour, completely unserved. A shuttle service was quickly established linking Eton with Slough. RT 4734 fitted with a well-produced slip board is seen in Brocas Street, Eton on the stand working on 18th May 1970.

Windsor was well served by Green Line coaches with routes 704 and 705 providing four coaches per hour via Slough to Victoria and beyond and the 718 running via Staines together with the cross-country route 725. Windsor's RF 239 is seen heading for Tunbridge Wells in Hammersmith Grove on 25th August 1962 running under the then redundant trolleybus overhead wires.

A high level of Green Line duplication between Windsor and London was provided during the summer season. Q 80 is seen standing outside Windsor Garage on Whitsun Monday, 14th May 1951, before working a relief journey to London on route 718.

On 28th August 1963 route 705 was speeded up to operate express between Windsor and Victoria with only 12 intermediate stops, running via Colnbrook By-Pass and Chiswick Flyover. Between Windsor and London white on blue express blinds were displayed instead of the usual black and amber panels. The coaches were also fitted with blue limited stop slip boards on the front and side. RF 79 is seen at Eccleston Bridge, Victoria on 28th September 1963 heading for Windsor. The vehicle was eventually converted into a towing bus in 1979.

RF 65 stands outside the pleasant frontage of Windsor Garage on 10th November 1963. Windsor Garage had been opened by London General Country Services on 1st March 1933 and like Dorking and Reigate which had opened in the previous year, was a vast improvement on the earlier East Surrey basic structure.

A major route renumbering exercise had taken place in October 1934 by which all northern area Country bus routes were numbered in the 300 series and the southern area in the 400 series. There was some indecision over the Uxbridge routes which retained their old 500 series numbers until December of that year when the 502 to High Wycombe became 455. RT 3511 lays over between trips at Uxbridge Underground Station on Easter Sunday, 2nd April 1961. The bus may be an extra which will be run as required.

Route 455A ran between West Wycombe and Wooburn Common although in practice the route was worked in two sections with most journeys terminating in High Wycombe. RT 4515 was photographed in High Wycombe Garage yard on 24th March 1962. Later, in October 1962, the use of route number 455A was discontinued and the journeys ran as 305.

158

On 23rd November 1968 route 455 was converted to MB operation but by that time the once regular service had been cut to a handful of journeys and local bus fares were charged on sections of parallel Green Line service 711. MB 96, heading for High Wycombe, approaches Beaconsfield on 28th May 1969.

A reorganisation of the department of the Operating Manager (Country Buses & Coaches) in October 1964 resulted in High Wycombe Garage being transferred from the North-West district to the South-West district. Therefore when a new route was introduced to serve new housing at Wycombe Marsh on 4th October 1965 it was numbered in the 400 series as 442. The route was initially worked by just one bus, GS 28, which is seen shortly after introduction on 30th October in Hicks Farm Rise where a loop working was performed. A bus stop pull-in bay has been provided but pending the installation of a post and flag a dolly stop must suffice.

Other than odd projections beyond Gravesend town centre route 489 running to Ash changed little between London Transport's re-organisation of services in May 1934 and the passing of the route to London Country in 1970. RF 659 is seen running through the Kentish countryside at North Ash sometime in the early 1960s.